Do You Like to Paint?

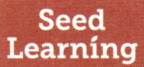

Do you like to paint?

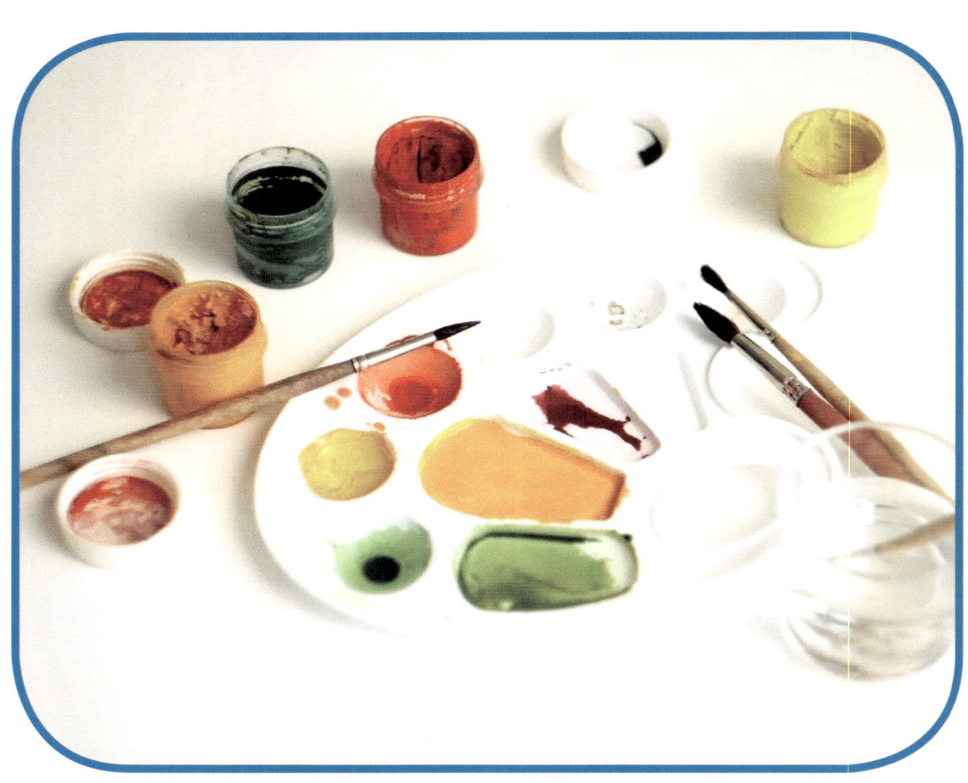

Yes, I do.

I really like
to paint.

Do you like to knit?

Yes, I do.

I really like
to knit.

Do you like to hike?

Yes, I do.

I really like
to hike.

Do you like to ski?

Yes, I do.

I really like
to ski.

Do you like to climb?

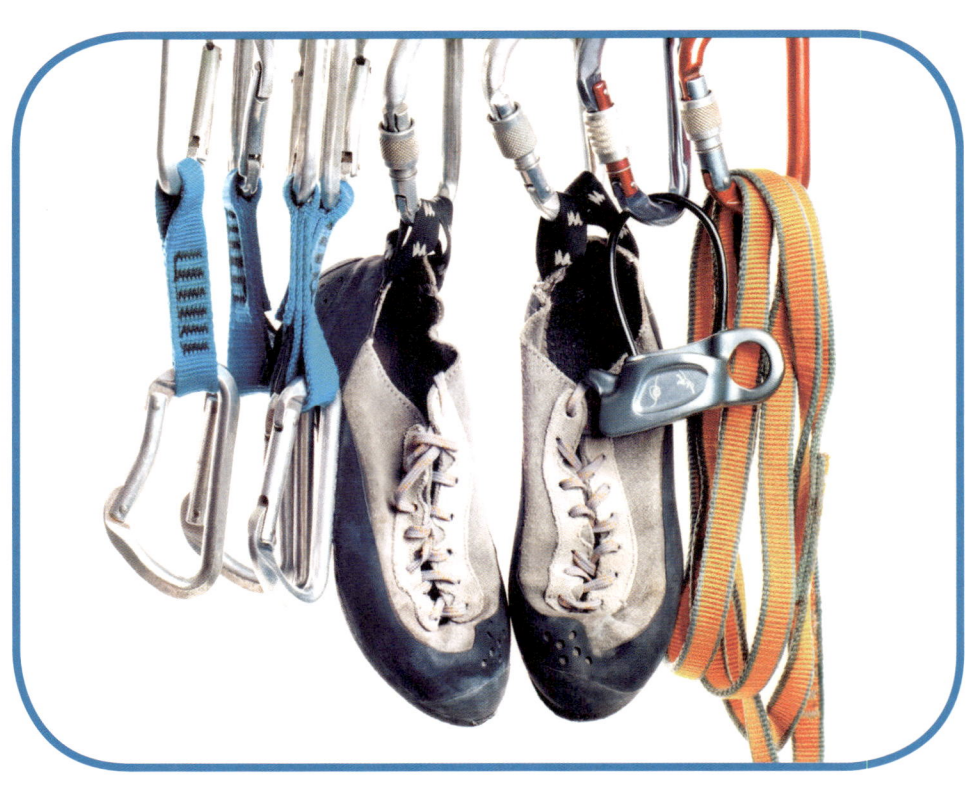

Yes, I do.

I really like
to climb.

Do you like to surf?

Yes, I do.

I really like
to surf.

Do you like to garden?

Yes, I do.

I really like
to garden.

Let's learn about Easter.

April						
Sunday	Monday	Tuesday	Wednesday	Thursday	Friday	Saturday
			1	2	3	4
5	6	7	8	9	10	11
12	13	14	15	16	17	18
19	29	21	22	23	24	25
26	27	28	29	30		

Trace the word April and circle the date.